FUGITT PUBLISHING GROUP PRESENTS

30 WAYS
to reboot in
30 DAYS
for the modern woman

DIONDA FUGITT

Copyright © 2019 Fugitt Publishing Group

Book design and production by
Fugitt Publishing Group

www.fugittpublishinggroup.com

ISBN: 9781798936344

For the mother who is making ends meet without her children seeing her in tears.

For the woman who has a nine to five.

For the woman who has the side hustle(s).

For the woman who is fighting battles in private, yet grinning ear to ear in public.

For the woman who needs just a little more time to herself.

For the woman who gave up on love.

For the woman who is unemployed.

For the woman who just finished college.

For the woman who is considering giving up.

For the woman who bares it all.

For the woman who continues to love after having her heart broken into pieces.

For the newly engaged.

 For the married.

For the single mom.

For the widow.

THIS ONE IS FOR YOU.

Life happens and we learn to deal with everything that comes our way. From our professional lives to personal lives, we grin and bare. How many times have you felt overwhelmed? Like the life you have designed was just too much to handle. There are various ways to deal with it. You can always resort to the unspeakable, crawl in your cave and hide – OR – you can take control. But how often do we put everything on the back burner and make ourselves a priority?

What if you decided to make it your daily duty to create a life where you're extremely proud of your personal growth? To take every negative moment and use that energy to give your thought process a makeover?

By the time you finish this book, my hope is that you feel rejuvenated. That you can turn on your *hell yeah* playlist and run the world. That you feel empowered. That you put yourself back on your priority list. That you realize that you are a beauty and a beast.

Table of Contents

one

GET A PLANNER
and use it

take time
to do
what makes
your soul
happy

unknown

If no one else has told you, let me be the first to say - whether you prefer digital or handwritten –

PLANNERS ARE AH - MAZING!!!

I am solely speaking from experience. I say this for multiple reasons but mainly since using a planner, I have lowered my chances of forgetting an important meeting, doctor's appointment or a school event (amongst a million other things).

Using a planner helps you force yourself to be accountable for your actions. Jotting down how much water you've consumed, and your daily habits will help you look at your lifestyle differently. Seeing that you spent a total of $45 on breakfast, lunch, and dinner on the go, may have you thinking twice before picking up your next meal. Creating a list in your planner allows you to prioritize and evaluate everything so you're prepared for projects, meetings, monthly tasks and anything else that needs to get handled.

ADDED BONUSES:

You can significantly increase your productivity.

Ever have downtime while at your little one's soccer practice? Peek in your planner and see what's on your to-do list that you can knock out. Make that dentist appointment in between cheering them on or call the dealership for your scheduled maintenance appointment.

Create ME time.

Ladies. This here is so important. Too often, we use the excuse "I don't have time". Somehow, we find time to browse social media, the web and watch reality television. After a long day of effortlessly wearing forty-five hats, I'm sure there have been times where you wanted to fall face first into your mattress after you've tucked your little nuggets in bed. Schedule a sleepover - at someone else's house - or even a drop off playdate. Rush home, safely of course, and run a nice bubble bath. Turn on some soft music. Grab a good book. Put your notifications on silent and vow to not check it until you're done. Take this time to focus on you and not other people's lives. If writing in your journal brings you peace, go for it. Pour your heart out while you have no interruptions.

Make an appointment to see a therapist. Mental health counts as "me time". Get a nice massage, a manicure, pedicure and/or facial. ME Time can even be a shopping trip. Yes - Walmart counts! Just make time for yourself, by yourself. Put it in your planner and make it happen!

It's great for brain dumping.

Every detail you try to force yourself to remember will be laid out for you. Trying to mentally maintain all of that data takes up your brain's bandwidth. If you put too much air in a tire, what happens? It explodes. If your phone or computer has reached its data capacity, we empty it in a hurry. Why cause yourself more stress when you can empty your brain by writing things down? You probably aren't aware of how many random pieces of information you mentally keep track of every day. Writing this information down in an organized format - that you can always locate - allows you to use your brain's extra space for more creative and productive endeavors. You may find that you sleep better because you have freed up some mental space.

But uhh - I buy the cute planners and never use them. That was the old you. She's gone. The new you starts today.

How to remember to actually use my planner

1 Push your makeup bag to the side and keep your planner with you all day.

2 Make it a habit of writing in it. Look at it in the morning to plan your day. Take a peek at night to check off your completed tasks and shift the unresolved to tomorrow's "to-do list".

3 Make it fun. No longer are we using the black executive looking planners. Get your favorite colors or design. You can even buy a basic one from your local Dollar Store and dress it up yourself.

two

MAKE UP YOUR BED

Each morning
we are born
again. What we
do today is what
matters most.

Buddah

Have you ever watched a show and wondered how they keep their rooms so clean? Have you ever wanted your room to look like a model home after you get home from a long day?

Make up your bed as soon as you get out of it! I can't tell you how put together I feel when I get out of the shower in the morning and I see my nice white fluffy comforter laid across the bed oh so neatly with my pillows sitting up like they weren't just mushed under my head for hours. It's such an accomplished feeling. It takes approximately four minutes and BOOM - just like that, there's one check mark on your to-do list. Simple right?

Once you begin making your bed on the daily basis, without over thinking it, you'll want more. You'll begin to feel like having your shoes put away, keeping your makeup organized and your dirty clothes actually going into the hamper is a priority. In the book, "The Power of Habit," author Charles Duhigg said, *"making your bed daily becomes a keystone habit, something that kickstarts a chain of other good decisions throughout the day and gives you a sense of taking charge"*.

Making up your bed as soon as you get out of it, may be just what you need to get the good energy vibe going!

Believe it or not, making your bed also builds integrity. Imagine a world where everyone took a few minutes to make up their bed. Now – imagine if those same people took a few seconds out of their day to pick up a piece of liter, to point someone in the right direction, or even took four minutes to help an elder take her groceries in her home.

No matter how late you may be running, making your bed reminds you to be in the moment. In that very moment, you may be thinking of ten other things, but your main focus is making sure your pillows are fluffed and your sheet is tucked.

Try it. Let's see what other doors may open for you!

three

SET WEEKLY GOALS

She turned her
can'ts into cans
and her
dreams
into plans

unknown

How are those New Year New Me resolutions coming along? Answer honestly and feel no shame! Studies have shown that only 25% of people stick to their resolutions thirty days in. Only 8% of them actually achieve them.

We can easily change that number by setting smaller goals. It's easy to say, "I want to lose twenty pounds in the next ninety days". GREAT! I'm rooting for you! Honestly, I am. But that one goal is more achievable when broken down into smaller goals.

Week 1 - Join a gym

Week 2 - Try out at least two classes (i.e. yoga & Zumba)

Week 3 - Try out two to three different classes (i.e. cycling & pilates)

Week 4 - Find a workout routine to try on your own

Week 5 – Weigh-in and make an appointment with the gym's nutritionist to share your overall goals.

Week 6 - (look we're already in month two! KEEP GOING!!) - Invite a friend to the gym

Week 7 - Find at least one class and stick to it

Week 8 - Dedicate specific days and times for the gym and work your schedule around it

Look at that! You are totally capable of passing the 25% of people who give up at the end of January! Go even further and set a goal for work, home, school, and/or your little ones.

Work: Organize your inbox into categories which will prioritize them. Go the extra mile and color code them.

Home: Make a chore chart....and stick to it.

(If you're a mom, make a chore chart for the little ones too! You're never too young to set and smash goals!)

four

THE FIFTEEN MINUTE WALK

Silence isn't empty.
It's full of
answers

unknown

How could this help me reboot, you may ask?

Walking is said to boost your mood almost immediately. Say good-bye to early moments of anxiety, frustration, and irritability. We're going to walk this one out. A quick fifteen-minute walk can help boost your circulation and increase oxygen supply to all your cells, which in turn gives you a quick caffeine-free pick me up and even healthier looking skin. Not to mention, you can get a bit of natural vitamin D.

There has been a study that proves those who are physically active are more likely to reduce depression symptoms. This study included those diagnosed with depression, healthy adults and medical patients without psychiatric disorders. The Lawlor and Hopker review proved that exercise was more favorable over drug therapy than medicine[4].

Making time to get out and move will improve your breathing, help you sleep better, help circulate joint fluid and strengthen your bones overall. Notice – I said **making** time. It's so easy to use the excuse "I have too much to do", or "I have deadlines" or "I'm not allowed to walk outside at work". Listen – this is your physical, mental and emotional health we're talking about. Here's my response to those excuses:

Excuse: *"I have too much to do."*

If you were to speak this nonsense to me, my reply may be: *"We all have too much to do before we die. Let's try to live one more day by taking a mental break"*

Excuse: I have deadlines."

If you were to speak this nonsense to me, my reply may be:

"Keep it up and you will be a dead line"

31

Excuse: "I'm not allowed to walk outside at work."

I understand some jobs are really strict, but very few don't allow lunch nor bathroom breaks. So, if you were to speak this nonsense to me, my reply may be: "Let your boss or manager know you are two seconds away from a breakdown and you need to take a breather. The truth of the matter is, if you died today or tomorrow (I pray you don't), your job will replace you. No questions asked. So – take a moment and make yourself a priority. If going outside is a bit of a stretch (or it's raining cats & dogs), taking a walk inside the building is still doable.

Taking a break to inhale life's greatest pleasure – fresh air - can get your creative juices flowing as well. So, to my fellow writers, authors, content creators, bloggers...GET TO STEPPIN!

Grab your bestie, colleague, partner and/or little ones. Encourage everyone around you to take a break. Hit the hiking trail, the mall, or even the sidewalk in the neighborhood.

I forgot to mention, there may be one downside. If you keep this up, you may need to go down a pant size...or two!

five

TWENTY FOUR HOUR VEGETARIAN

The habits you created to survive will no longer serve you when it's time to thrive. Get out of survival mode. New habits. New life.

unknown

Sounds crazy? It really isn't! It's not hard either.

***Please consult with your doctor, nutritionist or dietitian. I am not licensed to give health advice. I'm speaking solely from experience. ***

There are several benefits of being a vegetarian in general, but let's just start out with one day.

You get to try new recipes you may not have tried otherwise. Have you ever tried broccoli, cheddar & quinoa gratin? The funny thing is, a lot of meals that you eat on a normal basis, can be made into vegetarian meals. If you substitute one small factor, you get a bit closer to getting your vegetarian gold star. Make stuffed peppers - no meat - and voila! You've had a vegetarian meal!

Did you know that introducing more fruits, vegetables, legumes, whole grains, and healthy fats while reducing your meat intake can reduce most people's risk of various chronic health conditions: high cholesterol, risk of heart disease and cancer? If you don't like the idea of going 24 hours without meat, start with a meatless breakfast, lunch or dinner each day for 3 days. Plan meals that feature your favorites and have meatless options, such as lasagna, soup, salad.

The vegetarian (and vegan) lifestyle have become quite popular over the last few years. There are a ton of challenges, supportive groups and information available that could be of assistance. Believe it or not, vegetarians actually don't starve themselves nor do they just eat salads.

"OMG. We need meat for protein!!" For starters, the amount of protein you need can vary from person to person. So the need to consume meat to survive a protein deficiency is out of the question. The USDA Dietary Guidelines recommend protein make up somewhere between ten and thirty-five percent of your daily calories. But again, consult with your doctor for your specific needs. Vegetarians can get their protein from various beans, oats, nuts, seeds, as well as an array of fruits and vegetables. Believe it or not, a serving of greens has more protein in it than meat. Yes! It's true. Your broccoli and spinach can provide more protein than your beef and chicken.

I went on a weekend getaway to visit a friend in Georgia. I think it's worth mentioning that she is vegan, and I vowed to eat "her way" the entire weekend. I still can't find the words to explain the way my taste buds reacted when I had my first vegan burger. I assumed vegan burgers were made solely out of black beans. I was so out of the loop. We made a pitstop at a smoothie shop and she asked for three shots: lemon, wheatgrass, and ginger. She threw them back like a champ so I said, "I'll have what she had." No one warned me!! The wheatgrass literally tasted like blended grass shreds. Lemon and Ginger were just that. But REAL ginger. The after taste had my face jumbled up like a baby who ate a whole lemon. But after the research, I was glad I stepped out and tried something new. One ounce of wheatgrass has more vitamin C than oranges, more vitamin A than carrots and a host of other useful vitamins. It has over 70% chlorophyll, which helps oxygenate the blood cells and builds your system so diseases are less likely to get cozy. Lemon and ginger do a great job at reducing inflammation, aiding in healthy circulation, and soothing your digestive system. Then we made one last stop at a store which served vegan ice cream. I didn't taste it because I was completely full and nervous about what would happen after I had those three shots. Nonetheless, my friend had some and her ice cream sandwich looked like any other ice cream sandwich. I don't know why, but I was fascinated! Everything that I ate that weekend was simply amazing, but not as dramatic as I imagined. I thought fireworks would go off and I'd all of a sudden think clearer and my life would transition in one weekend. My eyes were opened to the endless vegan possibilities, but my life hadn't changed as much as I imagined.

six

MEAL PREP

Discipline is choosing between what you want now and what you want most

Abraham Lincoln

Since we're already talking food, let's chat about meal prepping. I'm sure the topic has crossed your conversation, news feed or inbox once in your lifetime.

So, what exactly is meal prepping and why is it brought up so much?

Meal Prepping is simply preparing some or all of your meals ahead of time. A lot of people have added meal prepping to their list of things to do while on their weight loss journey as portions can play a major role in such.

The benefits are endless, but let's start with a few:

You lower your chances of wasting food. HOW? Because you are consciously planning out your meals ahead of time and preparing them in portions.

Organized grocery lists.

How many times have you made a quick stop at the grocery store for bread and milk, only to come out with $250 worth of groceries? How many of those groceries go bad after sitting in the back of the fridge or freezer after two to three months? If you can say "none ever", I'd like to personally say "Congratulations". I have failed many times when it came to running in and out of the grocery store for two to three items.

When meal prepping, you know what each meal needs. If you know ahead of time that you're eating tacos on Tuesday and salmon on Wednesday, you will purchase accordingly in one store trip.

More health-conscious choices.

Once you notice you've written spaghetti and pizza for three days straight, you may be more inclined to add fresh vegetables to the menu for the next few days!

Save time (and money).

Instead of running late and having to buy your lunch, wouldn't it be nice to see your lunch already packed neatly in the office fridge? Typically, you can spend your full lunch hour getting to your car, out of the garage, sitting at traffic light after traffic light and in the drive-thru line only to order something you really didn't want but it was affordable and convenient. Having your lunch in the office with you saves time, gas and money you didn't need to spend. You may get lucky and be able to squeeze in a 15-minute nap.

Grab and go!

Enlist your little ones to pre-pack their lunches and snacks as well. Mornings run much smoother when lunches are ready to grab and go the night before. Have you ever wondered how the kids in your little one's class get the fancy looking character lunches? You know — the ones with the sandwiches cut into dinosaurs, butterfly clips that separate the grapes and the nuts. There's a chance those moms may get up super early to create their masterpieces OR they could prep their kid's lunches the night before.

Dear Mom readers,

DO NOT feel like you have to make character lunches daily. A smiley face on a cheese stick wrapping goes a long way. Believe me. I've tested this many times!

Meal prepping may take a few hours out of one to two days. The benefits are far more worth the time it takes to plan. Once you get the hang of it and figure out a plan to execute this on a regular basis, you may never go back to the "guess what's for dinner" game.

Meal prepping tips

1. Make a detailed grocery list
2. Schedule your days for meal prepping and packing
3. Choose your containers wisely
4. Make your slow cooker your best friend
5. Find your recipes ahead of time

seven

YOUR FINANCIAL HEALTH

Unless you control your money, making more won't help. You'll just have bigger payments.

Dave Ramsey

Upgrade your financial health by getting in tune with your credit and FICO score. Most people don't think anything of their credit score until they are about to apply for a loan or open a new account. Truth be told, there are months (sometimes even years) that go into preparing for higher approval odds. Your payment history makes up most of your credit and FICO score. Paying your bills on time and getting rid of inaccurate information isn't the only thing that stands between you and your future plans of a lavish life.

Keeping up to date with your credit report can:

Prevent (or correct) identity theft.

If you are up to date and in the know when it comes to your credit, you have a greater chance of catching identity theft as soon as it happens. Most credit tracking companies will send you notifications when a new account or inquiry has been added to your credit score.

Find (and get rid of) errors.

If you paid a bill that was in collections last year and it doesn't reflect on your credit report, chances are you can contact that agency and have them update your account. Let's say there's a credit card account on your report that is holding you back - but you never had a card with that specific company. Contact the credit bureaus immediately. If it's found that you have proven your case, it will be handled in your favor, and your score may rise!

Keep you informed of your approval odds before you apply for anything.

If you know your credit score is 465, you may not spend time applying for a million-dollar mortgage loan from your bank. Without knowing your score or the status of your accounts on your credit report, you can be blindsided by denials or terms less favorable than you expected.

Establish a budget. Another way to upgrade your financial health is by finding more effective ways to manage your money. For the first month, get a receipt for every purchase and consideration what you actually spend on groceries, gas, household products, entertainment, etc. Build your budget around that for starters and adjust accordingly.

Carry Cash. Swiping is so easy and those "processing" debits can be a pain. Carrying cash allows you to see what you can actually afford to order off the menu instead of hoping your card doesn't get declined.

Automatic Savings Account. If your bank offers an option to round your change up and add it into your savings account, by all means, take advantage of it. It's a great way to add money to your savings account without having to transfer it manually.

Quick tips:

1. Keep Your credit usage under 30%.

2. Being persistent with debt validation letters may be the best way to dispute accounts on your report (of course, depending on the account). Also, keep all deletion letters.

3. Boost your FICO score by signing up for Experian Boost. Yes! It's real! You can boost your score by registering and paying your utility accounts on time.

4. Enroll in a credit monitoring system. CreditKarma is said to be off by a number or two, but it is a popular one (no sponsorship here).

5. Create a payment plan with debt collection companies.

eight

LISTEN TO A PODCAST

Surround
yourself with
people who talk
about ideas and
visions,
not other
people

unknown

Do you have any favorites? Believe it or not, there are podcasts for almost every interest you can name. There are daily news talk podcasts, mystery & inside the minds of serial killer podcasts, shopping & couponing podcasts, beauty podcasts, comedy and reality podcasts and so many more. My favorites are podcasts that inspire and motivate you to be the best version of yourself and the ones that cover entrepreneurship. Two of my all-time favorite hosts (and guests) to listen to are Tony Robbins and Gary Vaynerchuk. They both inspire me and in different ways. After listening to either one, I'm ready to conquer whatever life throws at me.

Podcasts help exercise your 'mind's eye' as you have to imagine scenes and scenarios based on the description of the speaker. If your line of work requires you to pour into others, podcasts assist with refilling your glass. Face it – we all need to be poured into, why not receive it while you're headed into work, home, cleaning the house or out running errands?

Podcasts are also great for anyone who is an auditory learner.

The only downside that I have experienced with podcasts is this - I don't want to stop the podcast to get out of the car, so I'd sometimes find myself sitting in the car for thirty minutes after parking in front of my house or job. "Uh yeah, I'm late because I had to know what Gary V would say next after he told me to get off my ass and go for what's already mine". Imagine explaining that to my old boss. Ha!

nine

GRATTITUDE
&
COMPARISON
SSION

Before you try to put someone in their place, try putting yourself in their current space.

Dionda F.

Gratitude: the quality of being thankful; readiness to show appreciation for and to return kindness.

Face it. We all complain about the smallest mishaps in life. What if we went one full day without complaining? What if we showed more gratitude?

Gratitude is not only a way to fully appreciate life, but also a way to re-shape the mind. If we can re-wire ourselves to stop doing one small task (i.e. complaining), we can gradually move on to larger tasks. Instead of turning into a raging mad woman, try switching your complaints to compliments or moments of appreciation. If your best friend cancels your monthly brunch meet up, take that time to do something you've been putting off … like stopping by the post office. If you caught a flat tire in the middle of rush hour, thank the higher powers you weren't injured and have car insurance that covers your roadside assistance.

Try to catch yourself mid-sentence while screaming "I just cannot win" and switch to a compliment. "I am grateful for the many things I have accomplished". "I will have bad moments, but it's not a bad life." I'm not asking you to change your entire life and be Positive Patty every day of the year. I am simply asking you to give it a try for one full day and see where it takes you.

Instead of crying about the issue at hand and wishing you were in someone else' shoes, one full day of gratitude could encourage you to find a solution. Taking a step back and reminding yourself of your positive attributes could get you on the right track to attack the problem head-on.

Imagine if one day of gratitude took you from being in a box to becoming an open-minded woman? What if it gave you a different outlook on life which in turn gave you the courage you needed to finish that degree or start that business you've been dreaming of? All because you decided to stop looking at your student loans as a set ack and started looking at it as "well I already have the loans, might as well finish the degree!"

How many times have you turned your nose up at the lady in the grocery store line who has the newborn who won't stop crying, and the toddlers who are running up and down the aisle? Show a little compassion. Before stamping her as a bad mom, take into consideration that she may not have gotten any sleep for the past 24-48 hours because her newborn is inconsolably, her husband is in the army and her toddlers just woke up from their nap so they're super energized. How about having a small conversation with the little ones about their toys while mommy is loading her items onto the conveyer belt. How about asking if she needs help. Empathy & compassion go hand in hand and it doesn't take much to let another woman know you've got her back!

How can I show compassion and gratitude?

1. *Give compliments* to unexpectant friends, strangers, colleagues, and even the lady you sit next to on the train every Wednesday. I love giving compliments to strangers. I feel like my soul glows when I get to see someone's nonchalant facial expression transform into a smile to say, "oh thanks".

2. *Listen* to a friend in need. Actually, reach out to a friend who you know is having a tough time, or even one who you notice hasn't been them self lately. Just be there to listen, not to give advice – but just listen and remind them that you're there for them.

3. *Write a handwritten thank you note* to someone who has done something for you recently. To the mail carrier, the nurse from the ER, your instructor or anyone of your choosing. A handwritten note goes a long way.

4. *Jot down your blessings* in your journal, planner or even a sticky note. Daily. Weekly. Monthly. Just jot them down and read them frequently.

5. *Hold the door* just as you wished the guy before you did for you.

6. *Pay it forward* in any way possible. It doesn't have to be with a full ride scholarship. Next time you're in the drive-thru, ask the cashier if you can pay for the person's meal behind you. Can't afford the entire meal? No worries. Put five dollars towards it!

7. *Volunteer* at your kid's school, a family member's event or their church, a blood drive, a soup kitchen, your old school's event, or even a shelter. You never know – you may meet someone there who can enhance your life in ways you've never imagined!

8. *Share your knowledge* because there's someone who is interested in your story or how you became the woman you are today. If you have collected little known facts about history, share it. Share your findings on business, healthcare and even the government issues that a lot of people don't focus on.

9. *Smile* because it's free and contagious!

10. *Say Thank You!* It goes a long way. It lets the next person know they are appreciated and could possibly enhance their day!

ten

SMUDGE YOUR SPACE

When things change inside you, things begin to change around you

unknown

If you're feeling negative, depressed, mentally clogged or drained, it may be due to the stagnant energy you're surrounded by. There's an easy fix for this. Smudge your space. Don't worry. This is not a religious practice. It's actually an ancient ceremony in which you burn sacred herbs and plants, such as sage, to allow the smoke to clear and bless a space.

Sage clears out all of the negative energy and leaves you with a clean slate to reset your energy in. It has been said that sage is just as powerful as an antidepressant, can increase energy and could help enhance sleep patterns as well – thanks to the negative ions it holds.

Although it's not a requirement, I would suggest writing out your intentions if this is your first smudging experience so you can read them aloud during the process. What you want to put out into the universe is solely up to you.

It can be something as simple as "Clear this space of any negativity or stagnant energy so I may be more productive." If you prefer to say a prayer, that's perfectly fine as well.

How to smudge

For starters, give low/stagnant energy an easy way out, by opening your windows. Light your sage, then gently wave it in the air until the tip begins to smolder. Sage yourself by wafting the smoke towards your heart, over your head and down the front and back of your body. This is to cleanse yourself before cleansing your home. Hold the sage over a fireproof container at all times to prevent hurting yourself or burning herbs from falling on the floor as you smudge.

Next, starting on the lowest level of your home, move room to room and use your hand or a feather to waft the smoke into all four corners, where the ceiling and walls meet. I typically speak my intentions for my home aloud at this time.

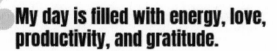

My day is filled with energy, love, productivity, and gratitude.

I am so grateful for all the beautiful blessings in my life and for all the wonderful things coming my way.

Move from room to room, typically clockwise, clearing out all the negative energy. Make sure you do not neglect the room corners, as they tend to collect and hold on to stagnant energy. Do not forget about spaces such as the closets, the garage, laundry rooms, and the basement.

Once you have smudged all areas of your house of your choosing, return to the starting point in your home and put you smudge stick into a bowl with sand (or allow it to sit until it burns out). Wait until there are no flames and the smudge stick has had time to cool down, then pack all of your supplies away.

Reboot your home by smudging as often as you like. I typically do so on a full moon, a new moon and anytime in between where I feel the vibes are "off". You know those times where you have a bad day at work and you bring that frustration home? I sage. When I feel the world is on my shoulders and I can't find a way out - I sage. Those moments where I feel defeated after putting my child in their place - yeah. I sage.

But I don't like the smell of sage.

No worries. There are various alternatives!

Palo Santo.

I just recently started using palo santo (Spanish for "holy wood"). When I was introduced to it, of course, I had a ton of questions to make sure it wasn't a piece of wood I could get in my own backyard. I was drawn to it after finding out it's from fallen branches of what's said to be a mystic tree. So, the tree is never cut down or damaged for profit! This particular tree grows on the coast of South America. Besides the physical aspect, palo santo differs from sage because it turns negative energy into positive energy, as sage clears out all negative energy leaving you with a clean slate. My favorite characteristic is the smell. Being as though it's part of the citrus family, it has a mix of pine, mint and lemon scent.

Smudge Spray.

If you prefer to skip the lighting process, you can get your cleansing in a bottle. It has the same effects as sage and palo santo. You can spray your way to higher vibrations.

Himalayan Salt Lamps. I have one in my bedroom and my home office for an extra sprinkle of relaxation. They are particularly great for those who work in highly stressful and tense environments. The warm salt crystals emit a high number of negative ions, delivering a more efficient ionizing effect and creating positive vibes. Negative ions are believed to produce biochemical reactions that increase serotonin, the mood chemical we all carry.

Crystals & Gemstones. Amethyst is known to help cleanse, promote peace and relieve stress. Tourmaline is a black crystal but is said to be the soul's bodyguard as it used for protection. The clear quartz crystal is used for clarity and focus. Your every need can be found in a crystal or gem. I like to hold mine during meditation or just randomly throughout the day, and sometimes even place them under my pillow as I sleep. Some don't believe they help manifest anything, which is completely fine. But if you just hold it or place it on your shelf as a reminder to stay focused, or be calm, or creative, then it has served its purpose.

eleven

LUNCH DATE WITH FRIENDS

Stay close to people who feel like sunshine

unknown

Time with your friends is just as important as time with your partner. **DO NOT** - I repeat **DO NOT** - stretch yourself thin trying to accommodate everyone. But when time allows, try to schedule a lunch date with your closest friends and/or family.

Spending time with your besties will bring out the best version of you. With encouragement to make the most logical decisions that benefit your wellbeing, your friends are the ones who will push you to live your best life. I'm sure there's one person in your group who isn't afraid to live on the edge. That friend may be the one who will push your growth. They are the one to tell you to start that business, date the one you've had your eye on, join that gym, go vegan...YOU CAN DO IT! We all need that one friend. It's therapeutic. Whether you all are discussing your goals or life's struggles, one friend has either been through it, currently going through it or has witnessed it before.

Making time with your inner tribe gives you time to be vulnerable in the middle of a supportive circle. Have you ever had a bad day at work, and met up with your friends afterward? Was it all smiles, sharing stories and laughing until you cried? Those are the best. Those few hours are needed and are nourishing to the soul.

Do you remember how important friends were when you were in school? In elementary school, everyone we sat next to at lunch was our best friend. Some of us had at least two different best friends between elementary and high school that we couldn't live without.

As adults, we can still make new friends and become the best of friends. It's not too late, as some make it seem. Believe it or not, having a good group of friends may extend your life. You laugh more. You cry more. You sing at the top of your lungs on karaoke night more, you travel more, and you let go of life's little hassles more when you have downtime. Being with your friends (male and/or female), can expand your mind, keep you on your toes and keep your blood pressure down...although sometimes they may raise it!

Don't let this world make you believe in the "no new friends" or the "I don't get along with females" mindset. At any age, any location and any setting, you can make new friends. Just because you didn't get along with females in high school doesn't mean you should shut down the idea of making females friends as an adult.

twelve

UNFOLLOW.
BLOCK.
FOLLOW.
ADD FRIEND.

If outside
validation is
your only
source of
nourishment,
you will be
hunger for the
rest of your life

unknown

When is the last time you posted on social media and checked back within five minutes to see how many people "liked" your post? Today? Yesterday? A week ago? No need to feel ashamed if you put this book down to check your likes. A lot of people are doing it as you flip through these pages. Are you triggered by other people's opinions, comments, or pictures when on social media? Have you ever felt like you needed to make a purchase to feel validated? Whether it be a plane ticket to Miami, a $550 pair of shoes or even an outfit from an online boutique? Do you notice you get jealous, upset, or annoyed when looking at someone else's page? If you find yourself comparing your lifestyle to the ones that you follow, maybe it's time to clean up your social media.

If you notice that you down talk yourself, it's time to change how you spend your time online. Down talking yourself doesn't have to be said out loud, to friends or to anyone for that matter. Your inner thoughts have the power to take control of your emotions. Down talking yourself and feeling as if you're less than will lead to stress and questioning your worth. We both know – you are worthy and neither of us needs social media to prove that.

I am not saying that you have to unfollow every celebrity gossip page nor every top model. What I am saying is that it's a good idea to separate from those pages for some time, just to give yourself a break. Exchange the gossip sites for a page that displays a hobby of yours (gardening, interior design, event planning, art, etc) Have you ever thought about starting a business? Follow a successful entrepreneur who has already laid out the blueprint to a successful business and is willing to share tips and tricks to getting ahead. Love fashion? Follow pages that take you behind the scenes of the designers. For every interest you have, there's a social media page that could take you deeper into your interest, heighten your excitement and may even help you get back on track with your life purpose. YES! I strongly believe we all have one. Yours may not be to sit and browse social media all day. I could be wrong. Who knows!

We log on as early as 8:00 am and we're constantly online until our eyelids are too heavy to hold. With the amount of time a lot of us spend on social media, why not use that time to enhance our lives? If you place encouraging and motivational role models in front of you, you're bound to be a force to be reckoned with in no time. You'd be the one to walk down the street smiling, throwing compliments like confetti, and feeling like you're on top of the world.

I actually did this and haven't turned back since. I used to follow a lot of reality tv stars. I'd watch the shows then follow them to keep up with their lives. To be 100% honest, I got nothing from following them. I was able to identify their families, get googly-eyed over their kid's clothes and how many cars they had. One day, I just decided to give it up. Not give up social media completely but rid the people who cluttered my life. Mainly, the celebrities and the pages who tore the rich and famous people's life to shreds. I substituted those pages for entrepreneurs I aspired to mirror, motivational speakers, astrology pages, home décor pages, nature, and healthy food pages. Now, when I log on to social media, I may still see some gossip here and there, but it's one page in between the thirty-five pages filled with inspiration and healthy living secrets.

Next time you log on try this:

Unfollow the mentally, emotionally and financially unhealthy pages. You know deep down which ones these are.

Block those who comment negatively on your post and pictures.

Follow those who uplift you.

Add Friends who you aspire to mirror or just simply admire.

thir
teen

CONTROL
YOUR APPS

Clutter is the
enemy of clarity

unknown

Can you believe at one point in time, we didn't know what an app was? Well, if you were a tech fan, maybe you weren't as clueless as most of us. We had the basics that the phone came with, but none of the extra stuff. In just a matter of a few years, we've gone from a few hundred apps to over two million apps. Ranging from daily exercise routines to financial advisory, banking, and stock management to how to keep your pet calm. We've got them all available at our fingertips. But do we really need them ALL?

A phone with cluttered apps says a lot about how a person's life is managed. It's time to delete the photo editing app you used once. While you're at it, toss those shopping apps you wanted to try out but haven't. Want to use them in the future? No problem. Start a list of apps you want to try out instead of actually downloading them. It won't hurt! There are more than a few reasons to delete unused apps and create folders to group apps that serve a similar purpose.

Deleting unused apps will lower your chances of having your information hacked. It's like having a random guy hanging around while you and your friends enjoy a nice stroll and have in-depth conversations. Eventually, that guy will get what he needs (a piece of personal information) and make a run for it. This day and age, hackers can remotely access your information if you have an outdated app. When you update an app, you're also updating its security features. Leaving an app to linger, puts you at risk. Let's not forget the apps that track you via GPS. Imagine how many unused apps know where you had dinner last.

Most apps were made to make our lives more efficient. How affect are they if we have to spend more than fifteen seconds finding them?

However you choose to organize them, just make sure you maintain the logic behind the organization. Whatever method you choose to implement – stick with it!

"Social Media", "News" "Travel", "Games", "Photography", "Finances", "Can't Live Without It" or give your grouped apps labels with emoji. Alphabetical order isn't a bad idea if you prefer to keep your apps lined up.

There's also your holding style. Pay attention to how you hold your phone throughout the day. Are you the type to hold your phone in your most dominant hand and use your thumb to navigate? Do you find it to be more comfortable to hold your phone in one hand and use the opposite pointer finger to maneuver? Or is it easier to hold it with both hands and use and use both thumbs? I type WAY faster this way.

Let's take a look at your phone holding style.

Suggestion: Add the most important four apps to the bottom of your phone. For example, your call log, internet browse, text messages, and the almighty camera! But of course, choose the apps you would personally best benefit from.

Suggestion: Keep the most used folders or app on the home page and second page. I have seen some who leave their home page/main page blank because of the background photo. Totally fine! But keep your frequently used apps on one to be most effective.

Suggestion: Choose your setup wisely. Those who use two hands tend to move faster than the other two. Yes! It can be great but can also cause you to run past the apps you need pretty swiftly. The folder technique tends to work wonders for the two-hand texter!

four teen

DECLUTTER YOUR SPACE

What I know for
sure is that when
you declutter -
whether it's your
home, your head, or
your heart -
it's astounding what
will flow into that
space that will
enrich you, your life
and your family

Peter Walsh

Why are you still holding on to the five oversized shirts with paint stains on them? Unless you plan on using them as a piece of your Halloween costume, please toss it immediately! Heirlooms and sentimental pieces are excluded from this process.

Start off slow by removing off-season items from your closet. If you can never see yourself wearing that ugly Christmas sweater ever again, add it to the donate box. Any items that haven't been worn in the last twelve months, toss them. They're taking up space that could be filled with items you can't see yourself without. The discolored, weird smelling, torn beyond repair items – toss them.

Next, get rid of anything that no longer fits. How did you feel the last time you wore that yellow dress with the broken zipper? Is fixing the zipper worth it? Did it squeeze you in the armpits? Did you feel ridiculous while trying to walk in it? Sale it on social media or one of the many apps or sites (eBay for instance) we can use to get rid of our unwanted items. Give it to family or friends who have asked to borrow it in the past. You know - that one cousin who always wants to borrow the shoes you haven't touched on two years. Call her and tell her to come to get them!

Decluttering your closet isn't just about getting rid of your old belongings. It's also a part of your transition. YES! You are about to step into the woman you've always desired to be. In order to be that woman, you are going to have to let go of what has weighed you down. A cluttered space will hold you back more than you realize. A cluttered closet (and any space in your home) can cause you more stress than necessary. Those who have cluttered spaces are more likely to have anxiety. To make things worse, the items you never wear are only collecting dust. Literally.

Take time to try on all of your clothes. If you aren't happy with the fit, toss it!

Decluttering can have some of us on edge. Anxiety can jump in mid-thought and say "na-uh, not today". This is where the new you steps up and pushes anxiety to the side. If it helps, set 15 minutes to the side and start slow...but you have to start!

Turn on soothing music (or music that will get you pumped), pour a glass of wine and make this a relaxing moment. Keep your positive thoughts flowing and get into the motion without telling yourself it's a chore. "I can't wait to see what this closet looks like when I'm done!" Keep the positive thoughts going and get yourself excited about the final results.

Decluttering your closet doesn't have to be done in one day. Give yourself a break when needed. Step outside for fresh air. Break it down to shoes today, tops tomorrow and pants the following day. It doesn't have to be rushed, but it must be done. If it helps – bring your girlfriends over, you know – like the scene from Sex in the City where Carrie Bradshaw was packing to move.

fif teen

THE BUBBLY

Spending time alone, getting to know yourself, is a beautiful act of self love

unknown

Run the water. Add bubbles. Press play on the slow jams…hold the lyrics. That's right. I said it - Absolutely no lyrics. Why ruin a good soothing relaxation session with tears? Let's admit – some slow jams bring back memories we don't need when we're trying to relax, right? This moment is about YOU, and only you. Turn on some soothing instrumentals and let your mind wander and create your own storyline or lyrics.

Although it's not recommended by some OB/GYNs to take baths on a daily basis, once in a while is doable. (Please check with your health care provider if you have conditions that may require you to skip this one).

Have you ever noticed that after you take a bath, productivity can fly out the window? That's because taking a warm bath gradually increases your body's temperature, which then rapidly decreases once you are out. This drop in temperature then signals your body to start producing melatonin. Melatonin is a hormone that's made by the pineal gland in the brain and helps control your sleep and when you wake up.

It's said that a warm bath can also stimulate the production of serotonin, the chemical in your body associated with happiness.

The hot water is a great way to loosen, relax and allow your muscles to heal naturally. Along with stimulating your blood flow and lowering tension, your bath water can also hydrate your skin.

Have you ever noticed yourself sweating in the bathtub? This is because your body temperature is at a point where it can allow itself to release toxins and boost your lymphatic system. If you feel yourself getting sick, a bath is a major key to getting rid of some of those symptoms. The steam from the bath works wonders for a stuffy nose and congestion.

There are way too many benefits to taking a bath that you can't help but enjoy.

six
teen

TAKE FIVE

Quiet the mind
and the soul
will speak

Buddah

Inhale the positive.

Exhale the negative.

Stress – also known as the silent killer – can disrupt sleep, cloud our judgment, promote depression and anxiety as well as increase blood pressure. You know how we tend to wake up and immediately start stressing out because we only have 15 hours left to get a million things done? Meditating for the first five minutes can help you mentally prepare to manage your to-do list and put everything else on the "maybe tomorrow" list.

Take five minutes of the beginning of your day to meditate. Mediation alone helps with age-related memory loss and can promote your attention span. Not to mention, it will aid in increasing memory, reduce depression, and reduces pain. Want to become resilient? Interested in controlling your emotions and improve your attention span? Want to gather your thoughts? Try meditating!

Trying out various styles of mediation suited to your goals is a great way to improve your quality of life, even if you only have a few minutes to do it each day.

If meditating is a struggle for you, YouTube has tons of guided mediations you could try and there are thousands of apps that can be of assistance as well. Guided meditations are led by a teacher or practitioner. In most cases, they are talking you through what to do to get the best results from meditating.

Inhale.
Hold it.
Exhale through your mouth.
Imagine a white light above your head.

Focus on that light.

Inhale.

Hold it.

Exhale through your mouth.

Imagine you're at the beach.

Listen for the waves as they hit the sand.

Inhale.

Hold it.

Exhale through your mouth.

seven teen

GIVE YOURSELF A FACIAL

Be the type of woman that makes other women want to up their game

Unknown

If you prefer, head to a spa and get the works. If money and time aren't on your side, no worries. Give your skin the lovin' it deserves in the comfort of your own home. Head over to your local drug store and spend twenty to thirty dollars on a few products (travel size is amazing) for your once a month treatment.

Always start with a clean face. Take a soft cleanser and clear your face of any makeup, lotions or creams. Next, use a facial scrub or exfoliant to rid the dead skin that builds up on your face, but won't harm the protective barrier of your skin. Exfoliating will revive your skin and bring back that glow that hides under the dull skin cells. There are tons of exfoliants and facial scrubs to cater to specific skin types. Oily skin, dry skin, and sensitive skin are all covered; just make sure you read the labels carefully. Rinse and pat dry your face.

If you want to go the extra mile, your face may appreciate a nice steam. The quickest, easiest way to steam your face is to soak a towel in hot water and wring out the excess water. Then lay the towel over your face. It should be warm enough to open up your pores, but not too hot so that it doesn't burn your skin.

Keep it on your face for several minutes, then proceed with your facial.

A facial steam will loosen the dirt in your pores as well as hydrate your skin. If you add in essential oils and/or herbs, you can turn your facial into a de-stressing session. Once my face is dry, I love to slowly massage my face with a light oil in a circular motion.

Facials (whether professionally or at home) can:

1. Reduce stress
2. Slow down the aging process
3. Rejuvenate your skin
4. Assist in eliminating acne
5. Eliminate white and blackheads
6. Boost your confidence

Need I say more?

eight teen

THE HELL YEAH PLAYLIST

A girl should be two things: WHO and WHAT she wants

CoCo Chanel

Honestly – life isn't always a walk in the park on a perfectly sunny day - well for most of us it isn't. Life gets hectic, stressful and sometimes we fall apart. An iced Caffe Mocha or a glass of Chardonnay can be a quick fix...OR... you can go the least expensive route and press play on your HELL YEAH playlist.

Sure you can turn on the radio, but who knows what you'll hear. A lot of songs now and days are senseless or extremely sexual – which won't boost your mood when you're upset with your partner. Then, some sad love songs are just played at the worst time.

A quick mood booster, or even a way to prepare yourself to have an amazing day, your playlist can vary in genre, artists or even theme. It doesn't have to be all GIRL POWER music. Just all uplifting music. Start a list with the songs that you NEVER get tired of, the ones that make you fist pump, the ones that take you from "ordinary" to CONCERT MODE in 3 seconds flat. You know – the songs that stop your tears and make you feel undefeated!!! YES! THOSE SONGS! These songs will orchestrate your mood, so choose wisely. They will be your Sunday soul food. You don't have to be a DJ or have the latest technology to create your HELL YEAH playlist.

The least expensive (and quick fix) antidote to taking control of your day, can be stored right in your phone! Press play and grab life by the wings. I have a couple of playlists and believe me, they change my mood almost instantly.

Firework – Katy Perry

Run The World (Girls) - Beyoncé

Titanium - David Guetta – feat. Sia

Love Myself - Hailee Steinfield

Hollaback Girl – Gwen Stephanie

Talk That Talk – Rihanna

Girl On Fire – Alicia Keys

Countdown – Beyoncé

Confident – Demi Lovato

Flawless – Beyoncé

Diva – Beyoncé

You Don't Own Me – G-Eazy & Grace

I Love Me – Meghan Trainor

As I'm sure you've noticed, I love how Beyoncé exudes feminism and embraces the whole girl power movement. But there's something about Katy Perry's "Firework" the really gets to me; like almost makes me tear up every single time I hear it.

Do you ever feel like a plastic bag
Drifting thought the wind
Wanting to start again
Do you ever feel, feel so paper thin
Like a house of cards
One blow from caving in
Do you ever feel already buried
deep
Six feet under scream
But no one seems to hear a thing
Do you know that there's still a
chance for you
'Cause there's a spark in you
You just gotta ignite the light
And let it shine
Just own the night
Like the Fourth of July

Katy Perry "Firework"

nine
teen

GET IN TOUCH WITH NATURE

The earth has music for those who listen

William Shakespeare

There was no typo there. Yes. I want you to take some time and get in touch with nature. I don't think there's enough emphasis put on getting outside and inhaling fresh air. There's plenty of praise going to exotic cities, big hotels and super large party cities, but not much attention is given to the adventures in our own backyard.

Have you ever seen pictures or heard stories of how people felt after camping or hiking? When the majority of them get over the bugs, how tired they were and their fear of bears, you'll get to hear about all the good parts. The parts where they soaked up the scenery, the scents and the pure beauty of the great outdoors.

As mentioned in chapter four, being outside gives you a chance to get your vitamin D naturally and lowers your chances of being depressed. It also gives you the opportunity to clear out your lungs, soak up negative ions and get some fresh air flowing in your system. If you want to go a step further, environments near the waterfall and the beach give off the best negative ions which help keep you calm. Do you know that scent of "freshness" after the rain or a thunderstorm? That's the best time to soak up the negative ions while at home. Taking time out to admire earth's most basic treasure, can also be refreshing and a great stress reliever.

Whether you choose to go rock climbing or just for a walk through the forest, getting outside is a great way to spend time with your family or spend time alone to clear your head. When is the last time you spent time with your loved ones without glancing at your phone or the television?

Live in the big city? No problem. Here are ways around that.

For instance:

- Go barefoot in the grass – I actually did this for many mornings and it felt great. To be quite honest, I felt like a kid again. I felt free. I was (well sort of still am) the type to think if I put my bare feet on the grass, I'd get bit by a molecule-sized bug that turned into a flesh-eating bacteria. So, to go barefoot in the grass, I felt like I had let my guards down and decided to actually enjoy life's little pleasures.

- Go for a walk through your local park - During lunch, after work, with the kids, with the dog or even alone. Walking in a mini forest with kids is kind of on the scary list (from my experience), so now I just walk on the open trail with my little ones and our dog.

twenty

SPA DAY

If you do not take control over your time and your life, other people will gobble it up. If you don't prioritize yourself, you constantly start falling lower and lower on your list.

Michelle Obama

I NEVER knew how important this was until I actually did it…in my 30s thanks to my sister! Sure, I've had the experience of getting manicures, massages, pedicures and my eyebrows done; but to get all of the above plus some in one day… WOW! The feeling of rejuvenation is priceless. If a mini vacation (or staycation) isn't in your plans, a spa day will be the substitute for a while.

When making your appointment at your local spa, health club or gym, be sure you're well aware of the different types of massages that are available. There are so many options: Deep tissue, Swedish, Sports, Prenatal, Trigger point, and the list continues. Your massage therapist may ask you a serious of questions prior to your appointment to see which option would give you the best results. The one thing they all typically have in common is they leave you feeling better than when you walked in.

I'm sure we can all agree that the right massage will make you feel like you're floating by the time your appointment is over. But behind that unbelievable feeling lies many benefits. A massage will help with anxiety, helps with headaches, soft tissue injuries as well as insomnia.

Most spas have become more of a wellness resort and offer more than massages. There are facials, body treatments and scrubs, nails, saunas and tranquility rooms at your luxury. There are also medial and mineral spring spas. With so many options, there's something for everyone and every reason to find what's best for you!

Budget tip:

Use one of the websites that have discounted rates (ex: Groupon). Find a coupon. Set a date. Sit back and enjoy. Home spa options are limitless. You can go to Walmart, Target, a dollar store, Amazon or your local drug store and purchase a few products to spoil yourself with. Don't forget the cucumbers, a fancy drink (wine, champagne even sparkling cider in a glass is perfect) and your favorite robe and slippers!

This could be an awesome opportunity to bring your girlfriends along and enjoy it together!

twenty one

TEATIME

Of course size matters.
No one wants a small cup of tea.

Unknown

Disclaimer: I am no tea expert by any means. I just enjoy it!

Now that we got that out of the way, don't come for my head when I say this - Coffee is great, but tea has way more benefits.

Teas of varieties have antioxidants that fight inflammation and prevent blood vessels from hardening. A 2017 study that was published in the *Journal of the American Chemical Society* found that green tea may assist in lowering the risk of Alzheimer's disease[3]. Green tea alone can improve brain function and assist in burning fat all in one cup. Sounds like a win/win situation to me.

Tea can lower your stress hormone levels, ease irritability and increase your short-term memory all while creating a calmer yet alert state of mind. Lowering your cholesterol and protection against heart disease are a couple of added bonuses along with giving an energy boost without the crashing feeling of coffee. "Excuse me – can I have a grande green tea to go please?"

Types of tea and benefits:

Peppermint Tea:

This tea is said to have antioxidant, anticancer, antibacterial and antiviral properties[5]. Peppermint tea can also help relieve indigestion, nausea and stomach pain. Ladies – Peppermint tea is amazing when it comes to morning sickness. I learned from trial and error!

Chamomile Tea:

One tea bag. Two awesome 'end of a rough day' benefits. Chamomile tea is a great way to calm your body down, especially on the unspeakable days. It's also is a great sleep aid for most. In one study of 80 postpartum women experiencing sleep issues, drinking chamomile tea for two weeks led to improved sleep quality and fewer symptoms of depression[6.]

Ginger Tea:

Some women use ginger tea as a way to cope with menstrual pain. It also is great to help improve circulation, fight cancer, reduce inflammation and improve food digestion.

Green Tea:

Looking for an energy boost? Green tea may be your go-to! Along with promoting weight loss, assisting with bloat and allergies, Green tea also helps lower your risks with certain types of cancers.

Black Tea:

Do you deal with anxiety? Black tea contains serotonin and dopamine which are great for controlling your emotions and concentration. So just imagine drinking a cup of black tea and a part of your brain yelling to the other side "Hey guys – time to bring it down a bit. We're going into calm mode". For those who deal with anxiety, black tea helps increase energy and focus and as an added bonus, it protects against diabetes.

Chai Tea:

 Made from a combination of black tea, ginger tea and other spices, small doses of this tea can help improve heart health and lower blood cholesterol.

twenty two

BEDTIME

There is virtue in work and there is virtue in rest. Use both and overlook neither.

Alan Cohen

Set a bedtime? HA!

In today's fast-paced way of living, not many of us fall asleep as soon as we lay our heads on the pillow. Our minds are racing - we're wondering if the house and car doors are locked, whether or not it's our weekend to bring snacks for the kid's sports games, planning for the next day and replaying everything that has happened in the last 20 hours of our day.

Then there are some, whose eyelids are closed and they are in a deep sleep somewhere between saying goodnight and their head hitting the pillow. If you are one of the lucky ones, setting a bedtime should come easy for you.

For those who suffer from insomnia or just need help getting some good shut-eye, we have to first understand that your body needs time to prepare to rest. Put the phone, tablet and any electronic device down as you're doing the opposite and overstimulating your mind.

Instead –

- Turn on relaxing soft music (I love my nature and Tibetan station on Pandora)

- Read a paperback book
- Take a bath
- Get a good eye mask. I don't know if it's because your eyes are being forced shut or the fact that its total darkness, but my eye mask is sent from the heavens.
- Pray and/or meditate
- Drink a cup of chamomile tea (remember? Chapter 21?!)

Do you remember your teachers reminding you to get a good night's rest? There was good a reason. While getting the suggested eight hours of sleep is great for your mood and can sharpen attention, it's also great for your memory, especially when it comes to learning a new task or lesson.

Have you ever been so stressed out, that you decided to sleep it off in hopes of waking up the next day with a batter attitude and clean slate? Good idea! High-stress levels can affect your cardiovascular health and sleep can lower your stress levels.

twenty three

THE VISION BOARD

Create the highest, grandest vision possible for your life, because you become what you believe.

Oprah Winfrey

Vision boards aren't just for after-school mentoring programs. Never were, never will be. A vision board is critical when it comes time to answer the million-dollar question:

WHAT DO YOU WANT?

A vision board is used to help breakdown, clarify, and maintain focus on specific life goals.

Millions of people say "I want a better job" - well, what kind of job do you want? Do you want to be a yoga instructor or a real estate mogul? What road do you plan to travel to reach either goal?

Have you ever heard of the law of attraction? It's explained as the ability to attract into our lives whatever we're focusing on or giving our energy to. So, if your vision board is designed to show where you plan to be in the next two years (financially, mentally, emotionally, spiritually, etc), you're allowing these things to manifest in your life.

Your vision board may be exactly what will keep you driven. Glancing at it while getting ready for work, may switch your "I'd prefer to stay in bed" mentality to "I need to be there on time to get this promotion – which will get me my dream car". There's no better feeling than knowing you set attainable goals and they are at your fingertips. Your only requirement is that you stay focused.

Now – let's be clear. You cannot, I repeat CAN NOT, create a vision board and think your life will change overnight. You have to put in the work. A vision board will be your constant reminder and will assist in manifestation. It will not do the work for you. My suggest – just a suggestion - stick to what your passionate about as it will make it easier to build a habit in the beginning.

For starters, decide what type of vision board you would like. You can have as many vision boards as you choose. If you want

to separate your professional life and personal life on two separate boards, go for it. Next, let's take the old fashion (and most preferred) route - cut and paste. You can print various pictures from the internet, cut from magazines, draw out your ideas, cut out letters to form words of your choosing, take it up a notch and add glitter and scrapbook stickers, family photos and even objects. It's your board. Personalize it to match your personality and most importantly – your aspirations and the path you're planning to take.

twenty four

THE STAYCATION

You can't say
YES to
everything and
not say yes to
taking care of
yourself. To not
say yes to health

Shonda Rhimes

stay· ca· tion /ˌstāˈkāSHn/

(noun): a combination of vacationing and staying at home

As soon as the word "vacation" comes out, all I can hear afterward is a money machine running nonstop. Staycations can cost, but not as much as a fully loaded and planned vacation.

Staycations can mainly be focused on "me time" ...or even "us time". Since the recession, a lot of people have, without regret, traded in airline and train tickets for days of exploring the world from their backyard.

But do I really **NEED** a break?

Yes. You do. So far, if you've noticed, I have pointed out the health reasons for many requirements in this book. Don't expect me to stop here.

Corporate America, entrepreneurship and side hustles along with daily life in general, can break you down – physically, emotionally, and especially mentally. A nice break from the day to day run around has so many benefits that you NEED.

After your next vacation (or staycation), you can return to your cubicle and brag about your:

- Enhanced sleep patterns: Get back on track to your eight hours of sleep. There's no enforced bedtime while on vacation, but there definitely isn't an alarm going off at 6:00 am (6:15 am, 6:30 am and 6:45 am) forcing you to jump out of bed and get ready for work. Sleep in as long as you'd like.

- Low chance of cardiovascular concerns: What if you told that vacationing could lower your chances of a stroke, heart attack or even heart failure. Would you make it a priority then?

- Enhanced productivity: Earlier, I mentioned that a walk around the block during your lunch break can loosen up tension and put your creative side in high gear. Imagine how productive you could be after returning to work from a long break? For every 10 hours of vacation time taken, productivity improves 8 percent.

A staycation can include a long list of activities such as:

Enjoying the water: waterpark, indoor pool or the beach

A day of the arts: pottery, painting and/or dance class, museums, DIY art projects

Adrenaline rush: Indoor competitive sports arenas, golf, an amusement park or (indoor) skydiving.

A day meeting the animals: Nature center, Aquarium, local zoo, camping

Romantic: Reserving a hotel room and ordering room service, cook a fancy dinner for two and have a movie date (at home or at a theatre) or even staying home and binge-watching your new favorite show.

twenty
five

FANCY
FEAST

You owe yourself the love you so willingly give to other people

Unknown

You know that feeling you get when you go on a date to a romantic restaurant with a white table cloth and a lit candle? Give yourself a piece of that every now and then.

Prep a nice fancy meal, not a quick go-to meal. I mean the ones on the cooking channel that you "oohhh" and "ahhhh" over when you see the finished results. Get the nice linen out and prep the table as if you were trying to impress a high-class critic. Bring out the fine china lady – you deserve it!

There's no need to wait on someone to treat you to a nice dinner. You deserve this on the regular, so why not provide it for yourself on the regular?! No need to wait for Valentine's Day, Mother's Day or any other Hallmark day. Select your day based on your schedule and your lifestyle.

After you've cooked this meal on your own (without the fire department involved), I'm sure you'll feel like an accomplished professional. Go the extra mile and get dressed up if you'd like. Pour yourself a glass of wine and enjoy your meal over some smooth tunes. There is absolutely nothing wrong with dating yourself for a change, even if you're in a relationship or married. Skip the awkward dinner questions and just converse with yourself.

If you have just gotten out of a long relationship, a nice meal for one is well deserved. You've spent countless hours pouring into someone else and pushing for the best. You have invested the time to understand how they think, why they react a certain way, how they can better themselves, how you can be the best for them, how you two can grow old together, helping them when they're down and being the listening ear in the late night hours. Now is your time. It's time to pour all of that lovin' back into yourself. It's time to cater to you.

Spending time alone in a setting where someone else is typically there will help you find your own voice, even if it's imagining someone else is asking you the most basic first date questions. Imagine your inner self holding the microphone and finally getting the courage to speak its truth. Spending time alone and reminding yourself of what you deserve will help you know what you're looking for in someone else. Also reminding you that there's no rush because you can serve yourself a fancy feast!

To my single ladies – if you can provide this for yourself, the next love who steps in will have to raise the bar. Thank me later!

twenty SIX

BRAIN DUMP

The page listens and does not judge. Therefore you can tell it anything without fear.

Unknown

A frequent brain dump will allow you to express all of your emotions in a safe environment. Journaling is also great for this.

Sometimes we need to let out a good ol' ugly cry, snot and all. The problem is, we're so wrapped up in balancing our day to day lives that we put our need to get in touch with our emotions on the back burner. Have you ever been in the car with someone and just wanted to burst into tears because of a memory that crossed your mind, but at that moment, you took a hard swallow and tried to change your train of thought? Then put that "everything is awesome" face on to prove you've got life together? Those moments build up and lead to us feeling drained and unbalanced. It even leads some of us into depression. Over time, and sometimes all at once, we feel like we're overly emotional, unstable and find ourselves feeling "lost". When in reality, it's because we have neglected our one on one time with our most personal and intimate thoughts.

Grab a blank piece of paper, pen (or your electronic device in the notes section) and just WRITE. Recording is a great alternative as well.

What doubts do I currently have?

What does your dream life look like?

What advice would you give your 22-year-old self?

What are you grateful for?

How would your friends describe you?

What are five things you love about yourself that you aren't complimented on daily?

If you couldn't fail what would you do?

What do you need more of? Less of?

What do you value most in life?

What does your ideal morning look like?

"In the next month, I want to_____".

What are you I afraid of?

What is something you wish more people knew about the person who are today?

twenty seven

PRACTICE THE TWO LETTER WORD

You can be a good person with a good heart, and still say "NO"

Unknown

NO!!

No, I can not help you.

No thank you.

Nope.

Na- uh.

Not today.

Looks at phone *turns tv volume up*

NO, I can not babysit tonight.

puts phone on silent

NO, I can not leave my house in my comfy clothes to pick you up in a non-emergency situation.

As women, we're naturally nurturers. We will give others our last...our last penny, our last two minutes, or last pinch of gas, our last loaf of bread, etc. Unfortunately, not everyone is ready to replenish the cup that they've emptied. This is why we have to rewire and remind ourselves that it's okay to turn down anything that is not refueling us.

Your "NO" will make time for you to put your plans in action, reenergize or just simply enjoy your downtime. Your "NO" will give you more time with your partner, your children or just simply more time to soak in the tub. You can't run the world when your tank is on E. OH…and another thing. Your "NO" does not need an excuse, nor does it need to be explained. "NO, I can't watch your kids because I have to work tonight". We all know you have a nine to five sis. No need to lie to reclaim your time. It's yours. Do as you please.

"NO, I can not work overtime". Yes, I totally understand it looks good when it comes time for your annual review, especially if you're working towards that raise. But honestly, how good will you be in that upper management position if you're burnt out now?

"It's only by saying 'NO' that you can concentrate on the things that are really important" (Steve Jobs)

twenty eight

QUIT COMPARING

A flower doesn't
think about
competing with
the flower next
to it, it just
blooms

Unknown

It sounds so easy. Quit comparing. POOF! Just like that, your daily self-destruction due to comparisons is now done and over with. If it were that easy, millions of people would've stopped doing it by now.

At one point or another, somewhere in between the one or ten hours you spend on social media, you've looked at someone and thought less of yourself because you don't have what that person has. It could be something they possess physically, mentally, financially or just their emotional state being portrayed.

Maybe it's the fit mom who posts pictures of her meal planning spread, her daily workouts and her cute little ones who seem to never have a hair out of place.

It could be a friend or family member who is always on vacation. Aruba on Tuesday and Bangkok on Saturday. It's tough not to be a bit jealous when you're eating a bowl of microwaved Raman at your desk of the job you dread going into every morning.

"OMG, she's so cute in that swimsuit. I will never be that skinny again".

"She is such a supermom. I wish I could balance it all so effortlessly like her".

"I wish my hair would shine like that".

"They're always on vacation. I wish my boyfriend would go with me somewhere".

We live in a time where a snapshot of everyone's life is available for our entertainment, whether good or bad. We take it upon ourselves to imagine their entire life from the few pieces we get daily. We see celebrities give amazing performances that leave us breathless and wonder how they do it and balance their time with their children and spouses and still make night club appearances.

What we don't see is the day to day hustle, their strict time management, the endless meetings, their chaotic daily agenda, and the nannies who are picking the little ones up from school because of the eight-hour dance practice for their upcoming performance they are committed to. Instead, we see cute pictures, quick videos made in between meetings and the gym and flawless performance.

Behind the scenes, the fit mom is planning her social media posts and grocery list when the kids are napping. She only gets five minutes to use the bathroom alone (per day) and the videos she posts may not happen the first take. She may have to edit seven videos to get that one perfect video and take twelve photos to get that one perfect shot.

Each and every ideal life you compare yours to is obtainable. Although it may take a little extra effort, some time management skills, some research, a resourceful team, and a great camera, it's not out of your reach. You may not get the exact same results in twenty-four hours, but your time will come.

Use what you compare yourself to as inspiration. If you want your home to look like your favorite interior designer, find the items you like and get to work.

Use your daily comparison as a guide to get what you want. If you love the way your favorite curly-haired diva makes her hair bounce with the perfect amount shine, leave a comment letting her know you love her hair then check out the products she posts.

Wanting to be the next skinny model with dark long hair and perfectly proportioned hips is fine. My only concern is this — will your soul be happy once you reach that goal? What if you do everything to be that girl and the guy you're interested in, still doesn't look your way. Will you be happy with your new improvements?

Instead of comparing, congratulate the ones you admire. "That swimsuit looks amazing on you". Genuinely wish them well and move on. Be motived, not competitive. Comparing yourself to others will only hold you back in the long run. While watching other people live their lives, you're missing out on living the best part of yours.

twenty nine

BE ANTI-SOCIAL

Putting my phone down, and picking life up

Unknown

What's the first thing you typically do in the morning after you open your eyes? Check social media – right? Don't feel bad. The best of the best do the exact same thing.

WHAT IF you tried to break that cycle? Try staying off social media until 10:00 am. Doing so gives you a chance to form your own opinion about today. If you're logging online and seeing "Ugh – Monday blues", you've already allowed someone else's reaction to their day have an impact on yours. A group of doctors recently surveyed 1,787 adults ages 19 to 32. Their study included the link between the use of social media and depression. Unfortunately, they found that the more time you spend on a social media site, the more likely you are to develop depression[2].

Instead – wake up, stretch, take a moment to journal, check your to-do list and plan a productive day, give yourself a deep moisturizing…. anything but get on social media. You can't use the excuse "My JOB requires me to post on social media." There is an array of scheduling apps for that sis! First things first – focus on yourself. Make YOU the priority. Not everyone else and their opinions, their lifestyle, nor their drama.

Have you noticed a lot of celebrities are taking a social media hiatus? As much as it is entertaining, social media is equally draining. If you're going through a painful breakup, social media isn't likely to assist in a fast recovery; but reclaiming your time is.

By giving yourself the time in the morning that you deserve, you're more likely to get in touch with the real you. You're more likely to reevaluate life and everything you have going around you. You're more likely to pray a little longer or thank the universe for such a beautiful morning. You're more likely to feel calm before you begin your day. When is the last time you stepped outside with a cup of coffee or tea and inhaled the fresh morning air? I'm sure you've used the time you could have been inhaling nature's medicine to scroll through your timeline before you've wiped the crust out of your eyes.

thirty

THE MONTHLY "B" WORD

A budget is
telling your
money where to
go instead of
wondering
where it went

Dave Ramsey

LADIES! Do you have your big girl panties on for this chapter? It seems when we talk about budgeting or money, it makes a lot of women cringe. Sorry to break it to you, but if we don't talk about, you'll never learn from it. Plus, who wants to be broke and financially unorganized all their lives? Uncomfortable conversations show growth, and ladies stagnancy doesn't look good on us!

A lot of us shy away from the "B" word because we feel it restricts us. Budgeting doesn't mean you can't go shopping. It may mean you can only afford to buy one outfit verses four this paycheck, but you may not have to cut it out completely.

No one is born with money management skills. It's a learned behavior. By the time we're adults, we are expected to be able to manage our money like pros. However, few of us are given the outline for financial literacy 101.

The basic goals are to pay our living expenses, manage our debt (good and bad debt), have funds saved for a rainy day and to maintain our finances to where we don't have to stress over money. Whether you use the envelope system, a budgeting software or a budgeting app, setting a monthly budget is a priority.

Rather than focusing on what some may consider the downside of budgeting, let's look at some of life's OMG moments that budgeting can handle for you.

What would happen if your car breaks down and you realize your insurance doesn't cover roadside assistance; or what if your dishwasher has sprung a leak? How would you pay for an emergency dentist appointment without breaking a sweat? The money you put away for a rainy day could save you in so many different scenarios.

How about we start slow. First, identify your income and expenses. Then separate your needs and wants. No. You don't NEED the $200 headphones and $500 shoes if you're on the verge of receiving a disconnection notice from your utility company.

Next, set a financial goal you want to achieve. Are you planning a vacation? Is there a payment plan available? How much do you need to enjoy yourself on the trip and have a little cushion for 'just in case' costs? After you think all of this through, then you can design your budget. Decide ahead of time what you'll use each paycheck for. If you receive two checks this month, will you save half from each check for rent/mortgage? Will you pay your rent/mortgage with your check closest to the beginning of the month or the check from the end of the prior month so your payment will be early?

I'm pretty sure you've noticed by now that I'm pretty big on setting goals and smashing them! Budgeting allows you to be in control of your finances, gets you prepared for potential future problems and helps you save a few bucks here and there by dodging late fees.

The Facts

[2]https://onlinelibrary.wiley.com/doi/abs/10.1002/da.22466

[3]https://www.medicalnewstoday.com/articles/321243.php

[4]https://health.gov/paguidelines/2008/report/G8_mentalhe alth.aspx#_Toc197778616

[5]https://www.ncbi.nlm.nih.gov/pubmed/16767798

[6]https://www.ncbi.nlm.nih.gov/pubmed/26483209

Made in the USA
Middletown, DE
23 January 2020

83647436R00132